TRANSFORMATIVE LEADERSHIP:
MASTERING THE HIDDEN DIMENSION

Companion Study Guide to
Transformative Leadership: Developing the Hidden Dimension

Joan Barstow Hernández & May Khadem

TRANSFORMATIVE LEADERSHIP: MASTERING THE HIDDEN DIMENSION

Copyright 2017 © by Joan Hernandez and May Khadem

Republished 2020

ISBN: 9798665280936

All rights reserved. No part of this book may be reproduced or copied in any form without written permission from one of the authors, except for the inclusion of brief quotations in a review, article, book, or academic paper.

CONTENTS

INTRODUCTION 1

THE CRISIS OF OUR TIMES 4
    AN OVERVIEW OF OUR AGE 4
    A PARADIGM SHIFT 4
    THE PROCESSES OF INTEGRATION AND DISINTEGRATION 5
    THE NEED FOR MORAL LEADERSHIP 6

MENTAL MODELS OF HUMAN NATURE AND SOCIETY 7
    INTRODUCTION 7
    MAN AS A RATIONAL ANIMAL 7
    METAPHYSICAL NATURE OF MAN 8
    COMPETITION AND ADVERSARIAL SOCIETY 8
    RACISM 9
    NATURALIZING THE SOCIAL ORDER AND INTERDEPENDENT PROCESSES 9

DOMINANT MODELS OF LEADERSHIP 10
    INTRODUCTION 10
    AUTHORITARIAN, PATERNALISTIC, KNOW-IT-ALL AND MANIPULATIVE LEADERSHIP 10
    COMMON DRAWBACKS 12
    DEMOCRATIC LEADERSHIP 12
    PROBLEMS WITH DEMOCRACY AS COMMONLY PRACTICED 13

A CONCEPTUAL FRAMEWORK OF TRANSFORMATIVE LEADERSHIP 15
    NEED FOR A NEW CONCEPTUAL FRAMEWORK OF LEADERSHIP 15
    SERVICE-ORIENTED LEADERSHIP 18
    PURPOSE OF LEADERSHIP: PERSONAL AND SOCIAL TRANSFORMATION 19
    MORAL RESPONSIBILITY TO INVESTIGATE AND APPLY TRUTH 20
    ESSENTIAL NOBILITY OF HUMAN BEINGS 21
    TRANSCENDENCE 23
    DEVELOPMENT OF CAPABILITIES 24

CAPABILITIES FOR PERSONAL TRANSFORMATION 26
    SELF-EVALUATION 26
    LEARNING FROM REFLECTION ON ACTION 31
    SYSTEMIC THINKING 33
    CREATIVE INITIATIVE 34
    PERSEVERANCE 35
    SELF-DISCIPLINE 36
    RECTITUDE OF CONDUCT 37

CAPABILITIES FOR TRANSFORMING INTERPERSONAL RELATIONSHIPS 39
    IMBUING THOUGHTS AND ACTIONS WITH LOVE 39

	ENCOURAGEMENT	40
	EFFECTIVE GROUP CONSULTATION	42
	PROMOTING UNITY IN DIVERSITY	55

CAPABILITIES THAT CONTRIBUTE TO SOCIAL TRANSFORMATION ... 58

	ESTABLISHING JUSTICE	58
	TRANSFORMING DOMINATING RELATIONSHIPS	59
	EMPOWERING EDUCATION	61
	ELABORATING A PRINCIPLE-BASED, SHARED VISION	62
	TRANSFORMING INSTITUTIONS	64
	UNDERSTANDING HISTORICAL PERSPECTIVE	65

INTEGRATING THE CAPABILITIES ... 67

	TRANSFORMATIVE LEADERSHIP IN THE FAMILY	67

EPILOGUE ... 68

	A WORD ABOUT AMBITION	68

REFERENCES ... 71

INTRODUCTION

This companion workbook and study guide was created to assist the process of transformative learning, upon which the book, *Transformative Leadership* is based. As outlined in the introduction of that book, this entails a six-stage process, the most crucial part of which is identifying and challenging our own unexamined assumptions – things we believe to be true, but which we have not scrutinized or measured against evidence and universally-accepted moral values. Since these unexamined assumptions, or "mental models", are not conscious, we usually are not even aware of their existence. When we encounter a problem, we try to find a solution without really understanding the source of the problem. It is similar to taking aspirin for a headache that is caused by something more serious, like high blood pressure. We treat the symptom without addressing the cause. This usually works for a while until the root cause creates a crisis not amenable to a simple solution.

Therefore, it is typically in times of crisis, when the flaws in our thinking become apparent, that we are forced to acknowledge them and adopt a more comprehensive understanding. However, we need not wait for a crisis. We can proactively acknowledge that our understanding is always incomplete and challenge our thinking through a process of collective inquiry where we actively identify, reflect upon and then scrutinize our assumptions. This is where a study guide can be useful, especially in a group setting where we can benefit from other points of view. In this companion study guide, we suggest questions for reflection and group discussion, together with activities that can stimulate a deeper exploration of the concepts presented in the book, *Transformative Leadership: Developing the Hidden Dimension.*

In order to make the best use of this guide, it is helpful to review the process of transformative learning: 1) providing context, 2) challenging mental models, 3) transforming our understanding through critical analysis, 4) adopting a new conceptual framework, 5) participating in a learning community, and 6) taking action. These stages are more or less sequential, although some stages may occur simultaneously.

When a problem presents itself, it is important to understand its context. What caused the problem? What else is going on? Is it an isolated problem or is there a pattern? Exploring the problem within its context has features of a "simulated crisis" that prepares us for deeper learning. It invites us to explore more deeply, however uncomfortable that may be. Providing context simply means understanding the problem in its own setting. For example, if there is disunity in the workplace, it is important to understand its many facets. Is there backbiting? Are people afraid of speaking up? What are the assumptions, or "mental models" that give rise to the situation? Are these true? What are the universal values that are relevant? Are they being violated?

We will address these different stages as we go through the various chapters of the book with questions and activities that will help our understanding and how we might apply what we are learning to improve our workplace and communities. The concepts presented in *Transformative Leadership* have been used successfully with many different groups and organizations throughout the world, especially in the fields of education, health, and youth empowerment.

The guide contains four types of questions or activities. Some are more relevant to certain groups and settings than others. Therefore, each study group is free to pick and choose among the questions and activities that are most useful.

Initial Reflection: We most readily remember new information when we can relate it to previous knowledge. The "Initial Reflection" has the purpose of stimulating discussion based on the participants' thoughts regarding the topic. This exchange of ideas can reveal multiple facets of the topic and prepare us to consider and integrate new ideas. This prior reflection may happen collectively when the group meets, or may be assigned ahead of time. In either case, prior reflection on the topic clarifies thinking and enhances learning.

Discussion Questions: Questions are suggested for discussion after reading each section. Some of the questions reinforce reading comprehension, putting emphasis on important concepts, while others require relating the concepts to previous experience. Still others require reflection on how to apply the concept in hypothetical situations and on what the impact might be. All these types of questions solidify learning.

Activities: The activities are divided into "individual activities" and "group activities". Both are essential in moving from theory to practice. The purpose of *Transformative Leadership* is not only to change our thinking but more importantly, to transform our actions through developing new capabilities. Participating in the activities serves as a first step in the application of our enhanced understanding. So it is recommended that some time be devoted to these.

Deepening our Understanding: Occasionally we have included references to books or videos by other authors that explore a topic in greater depth.

THE CRISIS OF OUR TIMES

An Overview of Our Age (p. 17-20 in the book, *Transformative Leadership: Developing the Hidden Dimension*)

Initial Reflection: Why do societies decline or prosper?

Discussion Questions
1. List four positive advances in the condition of humanity in the last 25 years.
2. How does disunity cause or aggravate the problems that we see in the world? Give examples.
3. What is the relationship between moral principles (or universal values) and current social problems?

A Paradigm Shift (p. 20-26)

Initial Reflection: What is a paradigm? Give an example. Is the world going through a paradigm shift at this time?

Discussion Questions
1. What is the difference between a 'mental model' and a 'paradigm'?
2. Give two examples from science that indicate a movement towards a new paradigm.
3. What are the main differences between the 'mechanical' paradigm and the 'organic' paradigm?
4. Why is it important to recognize that we are living in an age experiencing a paradigm shift?

Group Activity: Analyze the different stages of development in the human being. What are the attitudes and beliefs of each stage? What are the consequent behaviors?

	Childhood	Adolescence	Maturity
Attitudes & Beliefs			
Behaviors			

If we think of humanity as collectively going through these stages, where would we find ourselves now? What would humanity's collective maturity look like? Elaborate on your ideas.

The Processes of Integration and Disintegration (p. 27-32)

Initial Reflection: Can you make sense out of the chaos prevalent in the world? Are the various crises in the world random?

Discussion Questions
1. Explain the relationship between the processes of disintegration and integration.
2. Give concrete examples of what people might do (or not do) as they respond to the dual processes of integration and disintegration as: a) part of the problem, b) spectators, or c) agents of transformation.
3. Why can a relatively small group that dedicates itself to the process of integration have an effect disproportionate to its numbers?

The Need for Moral Leadership (p. 33-35)

Initial Reflection: What kind of leadership can help to solve the many problems confronting us? Where could we find such leadership?

Discussion Questions
1. What is the relationship between the efforts of an individual to live a moral life and his or her capacity to promote unity and justice at a collective level?
2. List a few problems that you see as high priority in your workplace or community. Are these just isolated problems or do others share these same problems? Ask yourself what caused these problems. Ask again what caused those problems. Do this several times until you arrive at the root causes. What are they?
3. Repeat the above exercise with problems in your country. Are these isolated or are they shared among other countries? Again trace the root causes. Do you see patterns?

MENTAL MODELS OF HUMAN NATURE AND SOCIETY

Initial Reflection: What influence do our ideas (mental models) about human nature have on our relationships with others?

Introduction (p. 37-40)

Discussion Questions

1. What is the most important understanding that we can take away from the study of Douglas McGregor (p. 38-39)?
2. When we speak of peace, unity and creating a better world, what are some of the arguments that people use to say that it is impossible? Make a table with two columns. In the left-hand column, list each argument. As you study the following sections, in the right-hand column write a response to each argument.

Man as a Rational Animal (p. 40-46)

Discussion Questions

1. What error does "Social Darwinism" commit? What is the consensus of scientists in this regard?
2. What characteristics have been most important for the survival and advancement of human society?
3. What negative attitudes are the consequences of determinism or fatalism?
4. What do scientific studies tell us about the development of pro-social attitudes and behaviors?

Metaphysical Nature of Man (p. 46-50)

Discussion Questions

1. Fill in the following table:

Assumptions	Positive Aspects	Undesirable Consequences
Innate Evil		
Inherent Goodness		

2. Explain how the understanding of man's dual nature maintains the positive aspects, while eliminating the undesirable consequences of these two assumptions about human nature ('Evil' and 'Goodness').

Competition and Adversarial Society (p. 50-54)

Initial Reflection: Is it necessary or beneficial to organize society based on competition and conflict?

Discussion Questions

1. Mention two arguments that people often give in favor of competition. Is there scientific data that refutes this?
2. Give examples in present-day society that show a gradual movement toward practices based on mutual benefit.

Deepening Our Understanding: Watch the video of Alfie Kohn speaking about the effects of competition: https://www.youtube.com/watch?v=b4c86SDW7FQ

Racism (p. 54-55)

Discussion Questions
1. How does racism negatively affect:
    a. the members of the race that is supposedly 'superior'?
    b. the members of the race that is supposedly 'inferior'?
    c. society as a whole?

Naturalizing the Social Order and Interdependent Processes (p. 56-59)

Discussion Questions
1. What is the relationship between mental models of human nature and mental models of society?
2. Give examples of negative practices that at one time were accepted as "natural" and were later changed or eliminated.
3. Why is it necessary to work on both personal and collective transformation simultaneously?

DOMINANT MODELS OF LEADERSHIP

Initial Reflection: What should leadership try to achieve in a group or organization?

Introduction (p. 61-62)

Discussion Question: How does each one of the three primary group functions contribute to the effectiveness of an organization? Give examples of the consequences of neglecting each one of these functions.

Group Activity:
1. Choose a group (organization, department) you are familiar with. Give concrete suggestions of what you can do to:
    a. Better achieve the goals and objectives of the group.
    b. Strengthen unity among its members.
    c. Develop the capabilities of the members.

    Discuss and then prioritize the different ideas. Consult on what specific actions you could take to apply the three most relevant suggestions in your group or organization.

Authoritarian, Paternalistic, Know-It-All and Manipulative Leadership (p. 63-69)

Initial Reflection: How do people often act when they are in positions of authority?

Group Activity: Divide in 4 groups. Each group presents a skit in two scenes, demonstrating one of these models of leadership. In the first scene the leader portrays the characteristics common to the style of leadership. At the end of the scene, something occurs so that he/she leaves (another meeting, a phone call). In the second scene, in absence of the leader, the members of the group express their feelings and reactions toward the demonstrated style of leadership.

After each skit, fill in the spaces corresponding to that type of leadership using the following table.

Type of Leader	Conduct that characterizes the leader	Reaction of the members of the group	Effect on the three group functions
Authoritarian			
Paternalistic			
Know-It-All			
Manipulative			

Individual Activity: Self–Evaluation

Fill in the following table, indicating in what circumstances or with what people you tend to fall into one of the four styles of leadership:

11

Leadership Style	With whom or in what circumstances do you sometimes use it?	What effects have you observed in the feelings and actions of others?	How would you like to change?
Authoritarian			
Paternalistic			
Know-It-All			
Manipulative			

Common Drawbacks (p. 69-71)

Group Activity: Choose one of the above four mental models of leadership. Imagine that one of you recently was named to lead a group that was accustomed to that style of leadership. What could you do to help the members transform their expectations, attitudes and habits and move to a shared, participative style of leadership. Give several suggestions.

Democratic Leadership (p. 71-74)

Initial Reflection: Is democratic leadership the answer to the above problems?

Discussion Question: Describe the benefits of each of the six practices that lead to synergy in decision-making.

Group Activity: Choose a topic for consultation about which you have to make a decision. Apply each of the six practices.

Problems with Democracy as Commonly Practiced (p. 74-79)

Discussion Questions:
1. Why are democratic elections not enough to overcome authoritarian, paternalistic, know-it-all and manipulative styles of leadership?
2. What problems occur in the decision-making process when there are sectarian interests and the formation of coalitions?
3. Give a concrete example of how the well-being of the whole benefits every individual.
4. What are some of the advantages of participatory democracy, compared to adversarial democracy?
5. Give three examples of problems that could occur in an organization when a participatory democratic leader lacks other capabilities, such as truthfulness, initiative, perseverance, upright conduct, vision, a spirit of service or the ability to learn from reflection on action.

Group Activity: Consider how you could introduce "elections without candidates" in organizations in which you participate. How could you protect yourself from 'self-promotion' while doing this?

Deepening Our Understanding: Michael Karlberg explores in detail the differences between adversarial democracy and participatory democracy in: *Beyond the Culture of Contest – From*

Adversarialism to Mutualism in an Age of Interdependence available through George Ronald, Publishers.

Also see his Ted Talk at https://www.youtube.com/watch?v=J0ZCAbYrQ7Q&t=2s

A CONCEPTUAL FRAMEWORK OF TRANSFORMATIVE LEADERSHIP

Need for a New Conceptual Framework of Leadership (p. 81-84)

Initial Reflection: Why is it important to develop a values-based conceptual framework of leadership to replace the mental models we have analyzed? What could be the source of these values?

Deepening Our Understanding: Many people, particularly in the West, struggle with the concept of "universal values." They are very suspicious of having values imposed on them and are leery of embracing values that they worry may not be their own. The following are quotes from different spiritual traditions, ancient wisdom, philosophies and contemporary thinkers. Have individuals take turns reading the different quotes.[1]

- "Each of us must start with himself or herself to evolve his or her consciousness to this planetary dimension; only then can we become responsible and effective agents of our society's change and transformation. Planetary consciousness is the knowing as well as the feeling of the vital interdependence and essential oneness of humankind, and the conscious adoption of the ethics and the ethos that this entails. Its evolution is the basic imperative of human survival on this planet." ~ Club of Budapest [2]

- "If people regarded other people's families in the same way that they regard their own, who then would incite their own family to attack that of another? For one would do for others as one would do for oneself." –Mozi, c. 400 BC (Ancient Chinese philosopher)[3]

- "Zi Gong (a disciple of Confucius) asked: 'Is there any one word that could guide a person throughout life?" The Master replied: "How about 'shu' [reciprocity]: never impose on others what you would not choose for yourself?'" ~Confucius[4]

- "The sage has no interest of his own, but takes the interests of the people as his own. He is kind to the kind; he is also kind to the unkind: for Virtue is kind. He is faithful to the faithful; he is also faithful to the unfaithful: for Virtue is faithful. Regard your neighbor's gain as your own gain, and your neighbor's loss as your own loss." –Lao Tsu[5]

- "Mencius said, 'First build the nobler part of your nature and then the inferior part cannot overcome it.' It is because people fail to build up the nobler part of their nature that it is overcome by the inferior part. In consequence they violate principle." Lu Hsiang Shan[6]

- "That which you hate to be done to you, do not do to another." Ancient Egypt[7]

- "Avoid doing what you would blame others for doing." ~Thales (c. 624-546 BC, Ancient Greece)[8]

- "It has been shown that to injure anyone is never just anywhere." ~Socrates[9]

- "One should never do wrong in return, nor mistreat any man, no matter how one has been mistreated by him." ~Socrates[10]

- "Virtue does not spring from riches, but riches and all other human blessings, both private and public, from virtue." ~Plato[11]

- "The (proper) punishment to those who have done evil (to you), is to put them to shame by showing them kindness in return and to forget both the evil and the good done on both sides." ~Tiruvalluvar, c.f. Tirukkuṛaḷ (Ancient India, c. 200 BC – 500 AD)[12]

- "Listening to wise scriptures, austerity, sacrifice, respectful faith, social welfare, forgiveness, purity of intent, compassion, truth and self-control—are the ten wealth of character (self). O king, aim for these; may you be steadfast in these qualities. These are the basis of prosperity and rightful living. These are highest attainable things….Treat others as you treat yourself. ~Vidura, from Mahabharata (Hinduism, Ancient India)[13]

- "I am a stranger to no one, and no one is a stranger to me. Indeed, I am a friend to all." ~Guru Granth Sahib (Sikhism)[14]
- In happiness and suffering, in joy and grief, we should regard all creatures as we regard our own self.— Lord Mahavira (Jainism)[15]
- "All things are our relatives; what we do to everything, we do to ourselves. All is really One…" "The first peace … is that which comes from within the souls of people when they realize their relationship, their oneness, with the universe and all its powers, and when they realize that at the center of the universe dwells…the Great Spirit, and that the center is really everywhere; it is within each of us." ~Black Elk (Native American)[16,17]
- "By making dharma (right conduct) your main focus, treat others as you treat yourself." ~Mahabharata (Krishna, Hinduism)[18]
- "…thou shalt love thy neighbor as thyself."~ Bible, Old Testament[19]
- "What is hateful to you, do not do to your fellow: this is the whole Torah; the rest is the explanation; go and learn." ~Talmud, Judaism[20]
- "That nature alone is good which refrains from doing unto another whatsoever is not good for itself." --Dadistan-i-dinik (Zoroaster, Ancient Persia)[21]
- "Whatever is disagreeable to yourself do not do unto others." --Shayast-na-Shayast (Zoroaster)[22]
- "Hurt not others in ways that you yourself would find hurtful." ~Udanavarga (Buddism)[23]
- "Do to others what you want them to do to you. This is the meaning of the law of Moses and the teaching of the prophets." ~Matthew 7:12 (Christianity)[24]
- "None of you [truly] believes until he wishes for his brother what he wishes for himself." ~(Islam)[25]
- "Blessed is he who preferreth his brother before himself." ~Bahá'u'lláh (Baha'i Faith)[26]

- The *Declaration Toward a Global Ethic* from the Parliament of the World's Religions (1993) proclaimed the Golden Rule – " we must treat others as we wish others to treat us" – and respect, justice, solidarity, tolerance, truthfulness, forgiveness, peace, compassion, love, and unity as core teachings of all spiritual traditions (signed by more than 200 leaders from 40+ faith traditions and spiritual communities including all of the world's major faiths – Baha'i Faith, Brahmanism, Brahma Kumaris, Buddhism, Christianity, Hinduism, Indigenous, Interfaith, Islam, Jainism, Judaism, Native American, Sikhism, Taoism, Theosophist, Unitarian Universalist, Zoroastrian, etc.).[27]

Group Discussion: Can you now agree with the following statement?
> *All people share the same fundamental human values, restated in different cultures at different times in history. Humanity has a common spiritual heritage, which is the foundation of ethical behavior.*

Group Activity: In the group, brainstorm values (or virtues) to which human beings aspire, such as love, compassion, truthfulness, etc. While we may define some of these differently depending on our culture (such as how reverence or courtesy is expressed), there is universal consensus on the importance of these values.

Individual Reflection: Understanding that there are universal values we all share, select 3-5 such values mentioned by the group in the previous activity, that can form a framework for your own personal and work life. List these and explain how each can help provide guidance for difficult decisions.

Service-Oriented Leadership (p. 84-91)

Initial Reflection: What is the most important service that you could give to another person?

Discussion Questions:

1. In your own words explain each of the five characteristics of service-oriented leadership (p. 85-86).
2. Relate each story in this section to one of the five characteristics of service-oriented leadership. Then share other stories from your own experience that demonstrate one or more of these characteristics.

Individual Activity:

1. Make a list of what you can do to better serve your family, your workplace and your community.
2. Explain how some of these acts of service help develop the capabilities of others. Share your insights with the group.

Deepening our understanding: Where does motivation for selfless service come from? Read Victor Frankl's book, *Man's Search for Meaning* or watch the YouTube video: https://www.youtube.com/watch?v=LlC2OdnhIiQ. Drawing from his own and others' experience in Nazi concentration camps, he demonstrates the power of commitment to a purpose that transcends the self. Extrinsic motivation – motivation coming from the environment in the form of rewards and punishments – results in behaviors that are short-lived. Intrinsic motivation that stems from satisfaction of the needs of the self results in behaviors that are mostly self-serving. While motivation that is inspired by a purpose greater than the self results in service that is transformative.

Purpose of Leadership: Personal and Social Transformation (p. 91-96)

Initial Reflection: What is the relationship between change in an individual's behavior and change in the group (whether at home, in the workplace or the community)? How does one affect the other?

Discussion Questions:
1. What is the purpose of personal transformation? Of social transformation?
2. Explain the relationship between personal and social transformation.
3. What are the benefits of participating in a "creative group" with others who are committed to the processes of personal and social transformation?
4. What are two basic requirements for transformation to take place?
5. What is the relationship between service-oriented leadership and personal and social transformation?

Individual Activity: Choose 2 or 3 goals for personal transformation that you can strive to achieve in the next three months.

Group Discussion: What can we do as a group to facilitate processes of social transformation in our family, workplace or community?

Moral Responsibility to Investigate and Apply Truth (p. 96-108)

Initial Reflection: What attitudes help us to investigate truth and learn more about reality?

Discussion Questions:
1. What is the relationship between the investigation and application of truth and the processes of personal and social transformation?
2. Explain your understanding of contingent truth and ideal truth.
3. How can we investigate contingent truth? Ideal truth? What tools can we use?
4. How does an understanding of both contingent and ideal truth lead to better decisions?
5. How does the process of collective inquiry or group consultation help us to understand truth at a deeper level?

6. How does the concept of moral responsibility presented in this section differ from conventional concepts of morality? What are the advantages of defining morality as the investigation and application of truth?

Individual Activity:
1. List principles to which you are deeply committed; then prioritize them.
2. Describe how you apply in your daily life each of the three most important principles.
3. Are you satisfied with what you are doing, or is there something more that you could do?

Group Activity:
1. Identify a challenge (or problem) that affects your group.
2. Investigate the contingent truth (facts, data, causal relationships) and the ideal truth (principles related to the topic and a vision of the desired result, which incorporates these principles).
3. Consult on the steps you could take to begin to move towards that ideal vision.

Essential Nobility of Human Beings (p. 108-112)

Initial Reflection: How do our assumptions about human nature affect our attitudes and actions towards others?

Individual Activity: Use this quotation as a guide: *Regard man as a mine rich in gems of inestimable value. Education can, alone, cause it to reveal its treasures, and enable mankind to benefit therefrom.*[28]

1. Make a list of everyone you work with. Next to each name, list their "gems."

2. Can you communicate your appreciation of these gems to each person in an authentic way? Carry this out and report on it at the next meeting.
3. Did you have difficulty in identifying the gems in certain colleagues? Choose the one that was the hardest. How could focus on this person's gems help you in moments of conflict or when having challenging conversations?
4. How will this help your own "gems" to shine?

Discussion Question: Complete the table below and answer the question.
1. How do our assumptions about human nature affect our thinking and actions?
2. How does our conviction about the essential nobility of human beings affect our relationships?
3. How does this contrast with the belief that people are motivated only by self-interest (the assumption underlying our current economic model)?

	Mental models about human nature	
	Human beings are motivated only by self-interest	*Human beings have capacity for nobility*
Basic concepts and assumptions		
Influence on our self-image		
Influence on our relationships with others		
Consequences		

22

Transcendence (p. 112-116)

Initial Reflection: What is transcendence? Why do we need it? How is it helpful?

Discussion Questions:
1. What are different ways we can practice and experience transcendence?
2. Describe three different situations in which the practice of transcendence would be beneficial. How might the outcomes change in each situation?
3. What is the role of "vision" in transcendence?
4. How does transcendence relate to each of the other elements of transformative leadership?

Group Activity:
1. Sit in a circle. Ask each person to share his or her reply to the following questions:
    a. In what situations of my life do I most need to practice transcendence?
    b. What helps me to achieve transcendence?

2. *Guided meditation*: Set aside 20-30 minutes of quiet uninterrupted time. Dim the lights, put on soft background music and ask participants to: 1) close their eyes and 2) relax with deep, slow breathing. Then, share the following instructions. After each question leave a short pause for the participants to remember and feel. When the mood is set, say the following:

    "Recall a time in your life when you were deeply moved – even moved to tears – by beauty, or by great acts of love, kindness, sacrifice, or nobility that you witnessed. Go back to that moment.
    a. *Where were you?*
    b. *What were you doing?*
    c. *Who was there?*

      d. What did you see?
      e. What did you hear?
      f. How did you feel?
      g. Relive that moment."

At the end, leave a few minutes of silent time. When you see people opening their eyes, ask them to write a reflection on their experience. Share some of the reflections in the group. This is an example of transcendence – connection to our higher self, to beauty and to nobility that moves and motivates us.

Development of Capabilities (p. 116 – 124)

Initial Reflection: Why is it important to develop capabilities?

Discussion Questions:
1. What is the difference between "passive morality" and "active morality"? Why is it necessary to develop capabilities in order to practice "active morality"?
2. Why are each of the four components of a capability necessary? What would happen if we tried to practice a capability without understanding the concepts? Without developing the skills? Without developing appropriate attitudes and qualities?

Group Activities related to the Conceptual Framework of Transformative Leadership
1. Think of someone whose leadership has influenced your life. What characteristics do you admire in this person? Is there a relationship between some of these characteristics and the elements or capabilities of transformative leadership?
2. Identify people on the local, regional, national or international scene who practice some of the elements of transformative leadership. Give examples from their lives that show their spirit of service, their efforts for personal and social transformation, their investigation and application of truth, their conviction of the essential nobility

of human beings, their practice of transcendence and/or some specific capabilities of transformative leadership.
3. Think of an organization you are familiar with. Identify the capabilities of transformative leadership that could help the members of the organization to have a more beneficial influence on society.
4. As you reflect on your learning using the consultation-reflection-action model, have you developed any insights that go beyond what is explained in the book? What are they?

CAPABILITIES FOR PERSONAL TRANSFORMATION

Self-Evaluation (p. 127- 131)

The capability of self-evaluation may, at first glance, appear deceptively easy. However, to practice it effectively, we need to go beyond giving ourselves passing and failing grades. We need to learn to evaluate ourselves without puffing up with pride when we get applause and feeling defeated and demoralized when we are criticized. Keeping our ego out of the process is key to effective self-evaluation.

Mastering this capability will greatly enhance our progress and permit us to develop all the other capabilities more effectively. We have to learn to measure ourselves, not against others, but against our own potential, recognizing that our life's journey is about learning to become the best that we can be. We can use role models to inspire us to strive, with full awareness that we have our own unique gifts and talents.

Initial Reflection: How can self-evaluation benefit us?

Discussion Questions:
1. Once we know our strengths and weaknesses, how should we use that knowledge?
2. How can we detach ourselves from ego in the process of self-evaluation?
3. Why is it necessary to have standards of excellence with which to compare ourselves?

Individual Activity:
1. *Self-knowledge (Strengths and Weaknesses)*. Carry out one of the two exercises below:
    a. Access the VIA Survey of Character Strengths through the following link: https://www.viacharacter.org/survey/account/register. Participants will need to register (free) to access the resources. The University of Pennsylvania collects data

for their research from people who sign in. The advantage is that this test is validated. The site also provides a link to a very useful website of positive psychology at University of Pennsylvania. Positive psychology was founded by Martin Seligman, author of *Authentic Happiness*[29], whose work has created a new movement in psychology to focus on well-being instead of pathology.

b. If you don't have an internet connection, you can take the assessment below to evaluate which of the following virtues you practice in your life.[30] Take into account the following:

   i. Your conscious understanding of the virtue and its existence.

   ii. Your efforts to put each virtue into practice.

If you are not conscious of the virtue and don't practice it, you should evaluate that virtue as 0. If you are conscious of the virtue and it is a habit, it should be close to a 10, with the recognition that there is always room for improvement and we will never practice any virtue perfectly. The virtues that you classify at 5 or below need your attention.

1.	Depressed	0 1 2 3 4 5 6 7 8 9 10	Joyful
2.	Cold-hearted	0 1 2 3 4 5 6 7 8 9 10	Compassionate
3.	Hateful	0 1 2 3 4 5 6 7 8 9 10	Loving
4.	Dirty	0 1 2 3 4 5 6 7 8 9 10	Immaculate
5.	Self-absorbed	0 1 2 3 4 5 6 7 8 9 10	Sociable
6.	Self-indulgent	0 1 2 3 4 5 6 7 8 9 10	Self-disciplined
7.	Cruel	0 1 2 3 4 5 6 7 8 9 10	Kind
8.	Thoughtless	0 1 2 3 4 5 6 7 8 9 10	Considerate
9.	Fickle	0 1 2 3 4 5 6 7 8 9 10	Steadfast
10.	Dissatisfied	0 1 2 3 4 5 6 7 8 9 10	Content
11.	Antagonistic	0 1 2 3 4 5 6 7 8 9 10	Cooperative
12.	Cowardly	0 1 2 3 4 5 6 7 8 9 10	Courageous

13. Rude	0 1 2 3 4 5 6 7 8 9 10		Courteous
14. Dull	0 1 2 3 4 5 6 7 8 9 10		Creative
15. Materialistic	0 1 2 3 4 5 6 7 8 9 10		Detached
16. Non-committal	0 1 2 3 4 5 6 7 8 9 10		Decisive
17. Indifferent	0 1 2 3 4 5 6 7 8 9 10		Empathetic
18. Prejudiced	0 1 2 3 4 5 6 7 8 9 10		Impartial
19. Mediocre	0 1 2 3 4 5 6 7 8 9 10		Excellent
20. Unsure	0 1 2 3 4 5 6 7 8 9 10		Confident
21. Unreliable	0 1 2 3 4 5 6 7 8 9 10		Trustworthy
22. Weak	0 1 2 3 4 5 6 7 8 9 10		Strong
23. Rigid	0 1 2 3 4 5 6 7 8 9 10		Flexible
24. Stingy	0 1 2 3 4 5 6 7 8 9 10		Generous
25. Dissatisfied	0 1 2 3 4 5 6 7 8 9 10		Grateful
26. Deceitful	0 1 2 3 4 5 6 7 8 9 10		Honest
27. Contemptuous	0 1 2 3 4 5 6 7 8 9 10		Respectful
28. Arrogant	0 1 2 3 4 5 6 7 8 9 10		Humble
29. Pessimistic	0 1 2 3 4 5 6 7 8 9 10		Optimistic
30. Aimless	0 1 2 3 4 5 6 7 8 9 10		Purposeful
31. Unfair	0 1 2 3 4 5 6 7 8 9 10		Just
32. Hypocritical	0 1 2 3 4 5 6 7 8 9 10		Authentic
33. Harsh	0 1 2 3 4 5 6 7 8 9 10		Gentle
34. Vindictive	0 1 2 3 4 5 6 7 8 9 10		Merciful
35. Extreme	0 1 2 3 4 5 6 7 8 9 10		Moderate
36. Vain	0 1 2 3 4 5 6 7 8 9 10		Modest
37. Disorganized	0 1 2 3 4 5 6 7 8 9 10		Systematic
38. Cynical	0 1 2 3 4 5 6 7 8 9 10		Idealistic
39. Impatient	0 1 2 3 4 5 6 7 8 9 10		Patient
40. Angry	0 1 2 3 4 5 6 7 8 9 10		Forgiving

41. Easily defeated	0 1 2 3 4 5 6 7 8 9 10	Persevering
42. Passive	0 1 2 3 4 5 6 7 8 9 10	Proactive
43. Self-serving	0 1 2 3 4 5 6 7 8 9 10	Pure-hearted
44. Gloomy	0 1 2 3 4 5 6 7 8 9 10	Radiant
45. Irresponsible	0 1 2 3 4 5 6 7 8 9 10	Reliable
46. Scornful	0 1 2 3 4 5 6 7 8 9 10	Reverent
47. Anxious	0 1 2 3 4 5 6 7 8 9 10	Serene
48. Idle	0 1 2 3 4 5 6 7 8 9 10	Productive
49. Deceitful	0 1 2 3 4 5 6 7 8 9 10	Sincere
50. Indifferent	0 1 2 3 4 5 6 7 8 9 10	Sympathetic
51. Thoughtless	0 1 2 3 4 5 6 7 8 9 10	Tactful
52. Intolerant	0 1 2 3 4 5 6 7 8 9 10	Accepting
53. Lazy	0 1 2 3 4 5 6 7 8 9 10	Industrious
54. Belligerent	0 1 2 3 4 5 6 7 8 9 10	Cooperative
55. Lying	0 1 2 3 4 5 6 7 8 9 10	Truthful
56. Lethargic	0 1 2 3 4 5 6 7 8 9 10	Enthusiastic
57. Foolish	0 1 2 3 4 5 6 7 8 9 10	Wise
58. Corrupt	0 1 2 3 4 5 6 7 8 9 10	Ethical
59. Agitated	0 1 2 3 4 5 6 7 8 9 10	Tranquil
60. Disloyal	0 1 2 3 4 5 6 7 8 9 10	Faithful

Whether you took the online survey or this one, identify the 5 virtues with the highest scores. These are your greatest strengths. They are also the ones that you should incorporate into your daily life as they will be a source of great satisfaction. The ones with the lowest scores are your weaknesses. Your task is 1) to use your strengths to overcome your weaknesses and 2) to choose work that is aligned with your strengths.

2. *Create a personal vision:*
    a. Identify 3 strengths and 3 weaknesses to focus on. Define how you would like to be after further developing each strength and overcoming each weakness.
    b. Make up questions, beginning with "How can I…?" related to what you can do to enhance each strength and overcome each weakness. Then answer each question.
    c. Make a diagram of a staircase with yourself at the bottom acknowledging your current strengths and weaknesses. Make another drawing of yourself at the top, indicating how you would like to be. For the first three steps of the stairs, write in some of the actions you have decided to take.

3. *Daily reflection:* The purpose of self-evaluation is to accelerate our learning and avoid repeating the same mistakes, not to flagellate ourselves or inflate our egos.
    a. Keep a journal to track your personal progress so that you can document your learning and refer to it, especially in times of difficulty. Each day ask yourself: "How did I do today compared with yesterday? How will I make tomorrow better than today?"
    b. When encountering difficulty, ask yourself, "What should I be learning? Is it a new concept, a skill, or some quality, or attitude that is missing in my life?
    c. Think back on a significant challenge in your life, perhaps even a personal tragedy. What did you learn? How have you changed? How do you want to respond to a similar situation in the future? Document your learning.

Individual Activity with Group Reflection: This activity is a hypothetical situation to awaken us to the important things in life and the value of bringing ourselves to account each day. Imagine the following scenario:

You have just seen your doctor who has given you alarming news. You have learned you have a terminal illness with only 3 months left to live. You feel fine and have energy, but your diagnosis is fatal. You are reflecting on your life. Take a sheet of paper and record your responses:

1. What are three things you have done in your life that you consider to be your greatest victories?
2. What are three things about which you have the greatest regret.
3. What are three things you can do TODAY to change your regrets into victories; three things you can do in the next 3 weeks and in the next 3 months.

Discuss in the group what you learned from this activity. How can we live each day with awareness of the priorities in our life? How can we use our regrets as fuel for learning and striving to improve?

Learning from Reflection on Action (p. 131 – 140)

Besides using personal reflection as a tool for learning, reflection can also be carried out collectively.

Initial reflection: How can we learn from experience in a group, so that we progress rather than repeating similar experiences? What can we do to eliminate contradictions between what we know and what we do?

Discussion Questions:
1. What is the difference between informative and transformative learning?
2. How does the "ladder of inference" help us learn the truth of a situation? It may be helpful to watch the video: https://www.youtube.com/watch?v=KJLqOclPqis
3. What are the benefits of using the learning cycle?

Group Activity: Use the learning cycle to reflect and learn from a group experience.
1. Select a significant experience shared by others in the group.
2. Elaborate a list of questions to guide your reflection on the experience, taking into consideration your unexamined assumptions. How can you make these transparent to others and courteously inquire about their experiences?

3. How did your thinking change as a result of the group reflection?
4. How will you use the new insights you have gained to alter your behavior? Make a concrete plan.
5. Implement the plan and then reflect on its success, examining what could be further improved.

The following tool can be used as a simplified scheme for ongoing group learning from action, especially when there are specific goals the group identifies and is striving for. It has been highly successful in monthly reflection meetings in businesses, resulting in unified action to overcome difficulties, especially when revisited and modified each month.

	Monthly Reflection Guide *Learning from Action*			
Goals	**Experience**	**Reflection**	**Conceptualization**	**Action**
No. 1	What was our experience this month? 1. Quantitative (data) 2. Qualitative (stories) 3. Is there missing information?	1. What did we expect? 2. Why the difference? 3. What did we do well? (numbers, stories). Why? 4. What could we have done better? Why? 5. How can we resolve these problems?	1. What have we learned? How has our thinking changed? 2. How will it affect our work? 3. What should we do differently? 4. What are points of consensus? (make sure all agree; call for a vote if necessary)	1. What *specific* actions will we take based on our learning? 2. *Who* will be responsible for carrying out the action(s)? 3. *When* is the deadline for completion?
No. 2				

No. 3				
No. 4				

Discussion Question: Contrast mental models with conceptual frameworks, explaining 3 significant differences.

Group Activity: Choose a subject where there are frequent discrepancies between people's discourse and action, or between the principles they affirm and their actions. Then, carry out the steps necessary to transform a mental model about that subject into a conceptual framework, using the four steps explained on page 138.

Systemic Thinking (p. 140-148)

Initial reflection: When we identify dysfunctional patterns in life that seem to repeat themselves over and over, what can we do to change them?

Discussion Questions:
1. Enumerate some differences between systemic thinking and linear thought. Why does systemic thinking lead to more effective solutions?
2. Give examples of an isolated event, a pattern and a generating structure.
3. Give a concrete example of the system archetypes of "Shifting the Burden" and "Limits to Growth".
4. What attitudes and qualities contribute to systemic thinking? How do they contribute?

Group Activity: Think of a significant problem that has persisted in your work or your community. Brainstorm about why the problem exists. When you have some insight, ask why again and again and again. Do this until you no longer generate answers. This is one way of getting at root causes and understanding patterns. You will notice that frequently the root causes point to the absence of one or more universal values.

Deepening Our Understanding: Learn about other system archetypes by reading *The Fifth Discipline: The Art and Practice of the Learning Organization* by Peter Senge[31]. Then identify examples from your own life experiences that demonstrate each archetype.

Creative Initiative (p. 148-151)

Initial reflection: What steps are needed to carry our good ideas through to fruition?

Discussion Questions:
1. Give an example of a routine initiative and of a creative initiative.
2. Select a creative initiative and give concrete examples of what might happen in each phase in order for that initiative to become a reality.

Group Activity: Think of an initiative that you have wanted to take as a group that hasn't been carried through to execution. Identify in what phase it "got stuck". What would the next phase be? What actions could you take to move the initiative to that phase?

Individual Activity:
1. You may wish to repeat the group activity you just completed with a personal initiative that you began but did not complete. Analyzing it in this way, helps us to understand what the barriers are and what the next steps might be.

2. *Making success out of "failure":*
    a. Make a list of some things you consider to be your "failures." Next to each, write down why you consider them failures. Were you justified in considering these "failures"?
    b. To allow creativity to flow through us, we often have to change our "self-talk." Frequently we sabotage our efforts by prematurely pronouncing judgment. This causes us to get stuck at the commitment stage, giving up when we encounter significant difficulties. Therefore, next to each item you identified as a failure, write down what you have learned. It is often at these points of challenge and difficulty that we break through with creative solutions.
    c. Next to each learned lesson, identify the next step you will take as a result of that learning.
    d. Change the title of this list to, "My Learning." A change in your own attitude will be the greatest stride forward to bringing your initiatives to fruition.

Perseverance (p. 151-153)

Initial reflection: What can we do at the beginning of a project to lessen the number of problems that will occur during its execution? What is the most positive way to respond to those problems that do arise?

Discussion Questions:
1. Describe two factors that contribute to commitment and perseverance in reaching our goals.
2. When we encounter problems, how do we balance perseverance with learning? In other words, if we come across "closed doors", when do we stop knocking and move on to a different door?
3. Why is it important to reflect on learning in this process?

Group Activity: Give an example of a real-life problem. Then offer two potential solutions, explaining how you would apply them in your example.

Individual Reflection:
1. Think of an unfulfilled dream you have. Write it down.
2. Why is it unfulfilled? Is it still a longing in your heart? Would its realization bring you fulfillment and joy?
3. Write down how perseverance can help you realize your dream. Is it impossible or just difficult? Be realistic.
4. Perseverance requires sacrifice. Is this dream important enough to you that you would sacrifice if you knew it could be realized? What sacrifice is required? Are you willing?
5. Motivational research has shown that the greatest motivator is a lofty purpose. Can you connect your dream to your purpose? Sometimes people even sacrifice their lives for a higher purpose. What is your lofty purpose?

Self-Discipline (p. 154-155)

Initial reflection: What are the benefits of practicing self-discipline?

Discussion Questions:
1. What is the relationship between self-discipline and achievement?
2. How does the exercise of free will relate to the capability of self-discipline?
3. Why is physical pleasure transient?
4. What is the source of true happiness? What does happiness research tell us?
5. What daily practices develop our capability of persevering in the practice of self-discipline?

Individual Activity:

1. *Select a goal:* Write down an important goal you want to achieve, and some of the actions necessary to achieve it. Then, explain why you need self-discipline to achieve your goal.

2. *Prioritizing and aligning:*

    a. List everything in your life that consumes your time (including the mundane acts of daily life). Next to each item, write down how much time you devote to it. Now make a list of all the things that are important to you. How much time do you spend on each one? Does the time you devote match the degree of importance to you?

    b. Now prioritize your list according to what is most valuable and important to you, including even those things you might now consider trivial after creating a priority list. The list should now have the most important (most valuable) at the top and the least important (or valuable) at the bottom.

    c. Self-discipline is often misinterpreted as a state of denial; this can create an unhealthy feeling of chronic deprivation – clearly not a sustainable state. However, if we look at self-discipline as a practice of knowing our priorities and never sacrificing something of higher value for something of lower value, self-discipline becomes much easier to master. With this understanding, write down how you will adjust your time commitment so that those things that are of greater value to you get the attention they deserve.

    d. Review your list based on this learning. What specifically will you need to forgo in order to achieve the goal you identified initially? This is the true meaning of sacrifice – giving up something of lower value for something of higher value.

    e. What actions will you now take?

Rectitude of Conduct (p. 155-158)

Initial reflection: Why is it important to base our actions on moral and ethical principles?

Discussion Questions:
1. What role do principles play in making wise choices?
2. Where might we look for those principles on which we can base our lives and decisions?

Group Activity: Think of a problematic situation that affects you as a group.
1. What responsibility do you have to take action in this matter?
2. What principles should you take into account in deciding what to do?

Individual Reflection: Think of a problematic situation that affects you as an individual.
1. What responsibility do you have to take action in this matter?
2. What principles should you take into account in deciding what to do?
3. If you witness injustice but are not directly affected, do you have a responsibility to act?
4. Will your action or inaction in some way add to the problem?
5. What is the definition of moral courage?
6. To what degree would you be willing to accept personal risk in order to uphold principle?

CAPABILITIES FOR TRANSFORMING INTERPERSONAL RELATIONSHIPS

Imbuing Thoughts and Actions with Love (p. 159-162)

Initial Reflection: What are some of the characteristics of love? Is it just a feeling?

Discussion Questions:
1. Explain Erich Fromm's concept of love.
2. Name some simple acts that demonstrate love.
3. How can we imbue our thoughts with love?
4. How does that change us? Can that change be perceived by others?
5. How does that change in thinking affect our actions?
6. How can we increase our capability of loving?
7. Can we love (or learn to love) people we don't like?

Individual Activities:
1. *Power of action*:
   a. What actions will you take tomorrow to show love to 3 different people in your life?
   b. Record the results of your actions.
   c. In your next group meeting share your experiences. What was the impact? On you? On others?
2. *Changing the narrative*: Think of someone who is problematic in your life. It is easy to have loving thoughts and show loving actions toward someone you truly love. How about someone you don't particularly like? How can you change your attitude? Your thoughts? Your actions? Is it possible?
   a. *Data*: Write down as factually as you can, interactions you have had with a person you don't like or for whom you feel antipathy. Be specific, identifying

conversations and actions as accurately as you can recall without interpretation or judgment. Write down the events as though they were captured by a camera. This is your "data".

b. *Story*: Now write down your thoughts and feelings in response to these events. This is for your eyes only, so be as truthful to yourself as possible. This is the "story" you are telling yourself.

c. *Assumptions*: What are the assumptions you are making? Are you attributing thoughts, feelings and motives to this person? How will you verify these assumptions?

d. *Verify*: Go back to the "data". Could you interpret these events differently? How do you think the other person interprets these events?

e. *Scrutinize*: What would happen to your "story" if you gave this person the benefit of the doubt and attributed only positive thoughts, feelings and motives to this person?

f. *Empathize*: What if you were that person with a similar background, life experience, and education? How would you behave? Can you feel empathy? Compassion?

g. *Adjust*: If you change your "story", is it possible to change your negative feelings? Can you substitute them with neutral or even positive feelings? Can these eventually grow into love? You may still not choose to associate with this person regularly, but can you let your feeling of compassion and empathy over-ride your prior judgment?

h. *Act*: With this new insight, what are some actions you will now take?

Encouragement (p. 162-166)

Initial Reflection: What are some effective ways to encourage others?

Discussion Questions:
1. How does encouragement help others?
2. What are some of the points to take into account when praising a person? Give an example.
3. What actions encourage a person?
4. What attitudes are necessary in order to give sincere encouragement?
5. How can you encourage yourself?

Group Activity:

Sit in a circle. On a chair in the center of the circle place several dozen small blank pieces of paper. Each person picks up a piece of paper, writes a short anonymous note of appreciation to another participant, commenting on a quality or capability he/she admires. He then folds the paper and gives it to the other person, looking him or her in the eye, saying: "I have a note of appreciation for you." He then repeats the process, writing a note to another person.

The process continues for as long as the paper lasts or the group wants to continue. During the activity, take care that all the participants receive a significant number of notes. The point of the activity is to identify and communicate in an authentic way positive qualities and capabilities (*the gems*) we witness in others. By doing so, we reach out to others from our higher self and connect with their "higher self". It is a celebration of our inherent nobility. At the end, everyone opens their notes and reads them. Discuss the impact on each person of writing and receiving notes of appreciation. What is the feeling of the group at the end? Was there a change?

Individual Activity:
1. *Taking action*: Choose 3 people whom you will see tomorrow (not including those participating in the workshop with you). Plan what will you will say or do to

encourage them. Carry out those actions. Afterwards, write down your experience. At the next meeting, share the reactions you witnessed. What was the impact on you?

2. *Learning to listen*: One of the most powerful ways to encourage someone is to show empathy. To do this in an authentic way, we need to learn what it is like to "be in that person's shoes". This requires being a good listener, showing genuine interest and gaining insight into how events impact that person. We are so used to experiencing the world only as it impacts us personally, that taking ourselves out of the center is not easy. However, when we are able do this successfully, however briefly, the feeling of validation and being heard experienced by the other person is a powerful means of encouragement. For the next few days, practice listening to learn how another person thinks and feels. Keep notes in your journal and share with the group at the next meeting.

Effective Group Consultation (p. 166-174)

Initial Reflection: How is group consultation different from other methods of decision-making?

Discussion Questions:
1. What are the distinguishing characteristics of consultation? How is this different from collective problem solving or simply reaching consensus?
2. How does consultation contribute to a more complete understanding of truth?
3. How do the principles of consultation reconcile the need for unity with the importance of sincerely sharing what each person's conscience dictates?
4. Choose two personal qualities that contribute to good consultation and explain their importance.
5. Why is it important that those who did not vote in favor of a group decision support it?

6. Identify 3 other capabilities of transformative leadership in which consultation plays a role, and explain how consultation helps in the development of each of those capabilities.

Group Activities:

1. *Initial Consultation*: Consult on a topic of interest to the group, trying to practice the 5 guidelines (p. 172) and 7 personal qualities mentioned in the text (p. 170-171). Then, evaluate yourselves, using questions, such as:
   a. Where could we have improved?
   b. Where could I have spoken up or remained silent?
   c. Did I dominate the discussion? Did I participate effectively?
   d. Was I courteous and and did I show interest in all the ideas expressed?
   e. Was I generally positive and optimistic?
   f. Did I demonstrate the relevant qualities and attitudes?

   Other members of the group act as "observers", taking notes and then giving feedback based on their perception of the quality of the consultation. In doing so, they should take care to avoid criticism, praising positive actions and giving constructive suggestions of what might work better. For example, instead of saying: "Mary interrupted a lot," suggesting: "Mary, it would be better if you waited until another person finishes speaking before giving your opinion." or "Try to remember to raise your hand before speaking." Depending on the level of trust, at times it may be better to give only generic factual feedback without mentioning names, such as tallying the numbers of interruptions, defensiveness, argumentation, etc., as well as the number of positive interactions observed.

2. *Initial individual reflection*: Write down the thoughts you had during the consultation. What did you notice? Be as accurate and truthful as you can.

a. Were you focused on the topic? Or did your mind wander to your own point of view?

b. Were you having internal commentary as others were speaking? Were you planning how to defend your position?

c. What were your thoughts about the different speakers? What were your thoughts about how they looked, how they dressed, the way they expressed themselves, the sophistication of their language, their status in society, their sex, their race or nationality, their age? Did you have judgmental thoughts?

d. Were there any emotional triggers for you? Was anything said that made you feel insecure, judged, not "good enough"?

These are important insights. We all have internal commentary and feelings when others speak. We need to own these and try to keep them from veiling us from the truth. As long as we are entangled in our own internal judgments and insecurities, we cannot participate effectively in consultation.

3. *Breaking down the different skills required in effective consultation:* Effective group consultation is a capability that is multi-faceted and challenging. There are many elements that go into becoming skilled in this important capability. First and foremost, we must be committed to the common goal of finding truth. We cannot do this unless we know how to communicate effectively – to listen with empathy and speak with gentleness. We have to listen in such a way that we gain insight and fill in the gaps in our own understanding. When we contribute our point of view, we must learn to do so in a way that engages others' listening capacities, instead of shutting them down. We must become aware of our own internal chatter and learn to quiet it down in order to truly listen to others with an open mind. We must tune into our own biases, prejudices, emotional reactions, and vulnerabilities, lest they hide the truth from us. We must do our best to make our "ladder of inference" transparent to others and replace our faulty assumptions with evidence-based data, and we need to

help others do the same. The exercises that follow focus on different skills that help us acquire and improve this vital capability.

a. <u>Effective Listening Exercise (about 30 minutes)</u>[32]: When we know how to listen, we open the door to genuine dialogue and empathy. We can only master this when we learn how to get our "self" out of the way, so that we can connect with another person on a deep level. This is probably the most crucial part of effective communication.

Purpose: To develop the skill of effective listening by learning to feel empathy, cultivate a genuine desire to learn from another perspective, listen and perceive in a more comprehensive way and detect verbal and nonverbal messages with greater accuracy.

Directions: Divide into groups of three, consisting of: speaker, listener, and observer. Each one will take turns in all three roles, 5 minutes for each turn.

Speaker: Choose a problematic experience you've had that you are willing to share. It may be a difficulty you had at work, with a colleague, with a friend, or in your family. Avoid the use of people's names or individuals that might be identified. If this sharing the story is too sensitive, you may wish to pick a hypothetical situation instead.

Listener: Review the guidelines for the listener in the table below and try to view this as an exercise of practicing how to learn from conversations with others.

Observer: Fill in the table below to see how many elements of "Effective Listening" the listener demonstrated and see what you can learn about how to improve as a listener yourself.

Scoring Guide for the Observer		
Directions for the Listener	Examples	Observations
1. *Show interest and the desire to learn:* Demonstrate encouragement by way of non-verbal communication and express a desire to learn.	Smile, nod, make eye contact; "I want to learn from you." "Tell me more…"	
2. *Try to understand the speaker's perspective and feel what the speaker feels:* Demonstrate interest and empathy, especially if a sensitive subject is shared; feel from the speaker's perspective.	Seek to understand not only facts, but feelings; "I can imagine how that made you feel."	
3. *Make sure to understand the facts:* Ask for missing information to help understand the objective information the speaker is conveying; ask for clarity.	In a courteous way. ask: "What? How? Why? When? Where? Can you explain further?"	
4. *Paraphrase:* Repeat what was said with your own words and check for accuracy.	"This is what I heard…. Is my understanding correct?"	
5. *Make sure to understand emotional content:* Explore what is not being said; perceive and ascertain the nonverbal messages.	"How did that make you feel?"	
6. *Reflect back the sentiments:* Identify what is conveyed of emotions or sentiments and ask for	"Is this how you feel?" "Can you explain why you feel this way?"	

clarification.		
7. *Summarize/Synthesize:* Summarizes the facts expressed and the emotions communicated; check for accuracy.	"This is what I learned…." "Is my understanding correct?"	

Group Reflections: (15 minutes)

1) As a speaker, how did it feel to be "heard"? What did you like? What were the challenges?

2) As a listener, did you find it difficult to concentrate ONLY on the speaker and not your own thoughts and feelings? What did you like? What were the challenges?

3) As an observer, what were your challenges? What did you learn from the exercise?

b. Effective Expression Exercise (30 minutes): This exercise will help us hone our communication skills for difficult conversations, as this is when it really matters what we say and how we say it. The key to success is keeping emotional content in check and learning how to make our communications safe. This requires that we genuinely care about the other person and his or her best interest as much as our own; this is what will also ensure the best outcome for ourselves. Since we cannot know what another person is thinking or feeling, it is safest to assume they have good intentions and also desire a fair outcome. In times of emotional tension – when we are afraid, angry, or hurt – we tend to feel victimized. We need to actively avoid this by describing those feelings in accurate words and examining them in a dispassionate way.

Purpose: To develop the skill of effective expression by learning to speak authentically, without fear and without anticipating negative feedback;

responding to others' comments with humility, courtesy, and gentleness. While this skill serves us well in any situation, the training scenario is a situation of conflict where how we speak can truly make a difference.

Directions: Divide into groups of three, consisting of: one person making demands, one effective speaker and one observer. Select a difficult conversation from personal experience or role-play a familiar topic that often creates conflict. Some examples are:

1) a teenager wanting access to the family car, feeling it is a right and is justified, while the parent is concerned about safety, lack of experience, setting precedent, losing control, etc.;

2) a teenage daughter wanting to go to a sleepover at a home that is unknown to the parent while the parent is worried about supervision, potential dangers, unsupervised internet, negative peer influence, etc.;

3) an older parent with excessive expectations from a grown son/daughter who has work and family responsibilities and cannot drop them all on demand;

4) a neighbor who does not respect property boundaries, is noisy, or in some other way infringes on the safety, peace and security of neighbors.

5) a boss who piles on work that repeatedly infringes on family responsibilities;

6) other typical scenarios of potential conflict.

The person making demands presents a typical point of view and defends that position to the best of his/her ability. The speaker tries his/her best to use the skills of effective expression to create a "safe space", to be "heard" and resolve the potential conflict. The observer uses the table below to see how many elements of *effective expression* the speaker (the one responding to the demands) demonstrates and what he can learn about how to improve as a speaker himself.

Switch roles until each has had the chance to practice skills of effective expression.

	Table for the Observer	
Directions for the Speaker	**Examples**	**Observations**
1. *Speak authentically*: Speak from your point of view and without fear. Do not attribute thoughts, feelings, or motives to the other person.	Begin sentences with "I", not "You." Don't tell the other what he/she thinks and feels or why he/she did something.	
2. *Give the other the benefit of the doubt*: Assume the other person is doing his/her best under the circumstances and you would behave similarly under similar circumstances.	"I would like to understand this from your point of view. Is this what you mean?"	
3. *Pay attention to the feelings.* This is your clue to the other person's "back story." The feelings can tell you more than the words.	"It seems you might be feeling _____. Is that correct?"	
4. *Verify your assumptions*: State what you assumed to be true and ask for clarification. Listen with an open heart to the answer.	"When you did _____, I assumed you _____. Is that correct?" "Could you help me understand what led you to say (or do) _____."	

5. *Make your own thinking process transparent:* Explain what you were thinking when you said or did something to escalate the conflict while avoiding defensiveness.	"I said _____ because of _____. I did _____ because I thought____"	
6. *Expose your feelings:* Be willing to be vulnerable. Explain how you feel.	"I am frightened about _____. I am worried about _____."	
7. *Avoid defending your position:* If you think you were not heard correctly, clarify with courtesy, but do not defend.	"I think you may have misunderstood my intention. This is what I would like to clarify_____." "	
8. *Make it safe:* You must genuinely care about the other person and his/her best interest. Speak in a soft tone of voice with kindness, courtesy and respect. Do not raise your voice; control your emotions. If you feel something is unjust, say so in a factual respectful way.	Relax your body. Soften your expression. Abandon your anger. Show that you are willing to hear without negative reaction. "Please explain how you feel, I want to understand." "I know we can find a mutually satisfactory outcome." "I feel your words don't accurately represent my perspective. I feel you misinterpreted my statements."	

Group Reflection about Effective Communication (Listening and Speaking): (15 minutes)
1) As a speaker, were you able to keep your emotions under control? Did you feel judged? Did your own fears create barriers in communication? Were you able to voice your fears with kindness and courtesy?
2) As a speaker, how did it feel to be "heard"?
3) As a listener, did you find it difficult to concentrate ONLY on the speaker and not jump to your own thoughts and feelings?
4) What were your challenges as a speaker? As a listener? As observer?
5) What did you learn? Will this skill help you in times of conflict?

c. <u>Fearless Expression and Deep Listening: Blindfold Exercise</u> (30-40 minutes)[33]. In a group setting, we are often influenced and/or distracted by visual input. Removing these extraneous inputs can transform what we hear and how we respond. This exercise attempts to do that so that there is more focus on the speaker, with fewer interruptions and blurring of boundaries between people. Removing excess input not relevant to the topic under discussion often results in less internal chatter and better listening.

Purpose: To express ourselves without being influenced by who is listening, what they look like, what their position is, or how old they are. Also missing are the usual distractions of other people's movements and body language. The only focus will be on the ideas we wish to share and the words we hear. This helps us overcome our tendencies to allow "mental models" to interfere with our capacity to consult effectively.

Directions: This requires an atmosphere where people feel safe and free to speak. Everyone wears a blindfold except the timekeeper. Ask the room to become silent and wait until there is true stillness (It may take 2 minutes or more). People are free to speak about anything they wish, but each one should make a contribution to the discussion. The purpose is not to arrive at a decision or resolve a problem, although this may spontaneously happen. The goal is to notice what happens when the usual distractions are removed, listening and speaking without fear. Continue for 20 minutes or more. When the time is up, the facilitator quietly announces that the participants should finish their discussion. They can then remove their blindfolds.

Group Reflection: What was your experience?
1) Were you able to focus only on the message and not the personality?
2) What were your challenges? Was it easier or harder to express yourself blind-folded? Why?
3) How did you feel: safer or more vulnerable?
4) What did you learn about yourself? About others?
5) What else would you like to share about the exercise?

d. Putting it all together: "Fishbowl" Consultation (about 2 hours)[34]. Consultation is more than effective communication. While effective listening and effective expression are critical skills for communication, consultation is a channel through which those skills can lead to discovery of truth through collective wisdom, enhanced understanding, peak creativity, and a level of unity that is otherwise elusive.

Directions: The topic for discussion should be a difficult one. Choose something relevant to the group that needs to be brought to the surface and resolved.

Part 1: Establish Rapport (5 minutes): Choose a partner from whom you do not mind getting feedback. Sit in pairs and ask each other these questions:
1) What is your vision of a satisfactory outcome?
2) What qualities and attitudes do you need for successful consultation?
3) What opinions do you have (as an individual) about this topic?
4) What observable data (facts, not opinions) can you bring to the group's consultation?

5) How willing are you to change your mind?

The purpose is to assure that both partners understand each other's goals for consultation, the necessary attributes and attitudes that are needed, assumptions they hold that may bias their search for truth, and their willingness to learn.

Part 2: Group A in the Center (15 minutes): Chairs are arranged in two circles (one inside the other; all facing the center) with no tables. From each pair, one partner joins the inner circle (Group A) and one the outer circle (Group B). These two groups will take turns talking and observing.

1) Members of Group A will begin the consultation, following the guidelines for consultation, understanding the process they are seeking, and checking their own internal state.

2) Members of Group B take the role of observer/coach. They sit in the outer row, but exactly opposite their partners, so they can see their partner's face and hear him/her easily. They take notes about their partner only, recording specific instances (including comments) that illustrate their partner's skill in effective consultation, using the following questions as guidelines:

   a) When expressing him/herself, how often did your partner:
   - State his/her opinion and ideas so clearly that those listening could picture them in their own minds and so gently that there was no need for defense.
   - Offer the assumptions on which their opinions and ideas are built.
   - Provide observable data (facts only, not anecdotes or opinions) to support the line of reasoning.
   - Invite others in the group to add their ideas.

- Avoid defensiveness when questioned.

b) When listening, how often did your partner:

- Ask questions about others' assumptions and data without triggering defensiveness?
- Ask questions which increased the group's understanding of someone's opinions?
- Listen without judgment (attentively, and without interruptions) as others spoke?

Part 3: First Critique (5 minutes): Return to pairs. The observer/coach reviews feedback notes with the talker. When giving feedback, use the same courtesy, consideration and clarity as you would in consultation. For example, instead of saying, "You were really defensive," your feedback will be better received if you say, "I interpreted this comment, ----------, as being defensive." The specific example is much more helpful, less judgmental, and will be better received.

Part 4: New Round of Consultation with Critique (20 minutes): Group A returns to the inner circle and resumes consultation on the same subject. Again the partners from Group B sit opposite, observe and take notes as before. After the consultation, the partners return to their pairs for feedback. This time the focus is on what has changed. The purpose is to build competence, not to see what was done wrong.

Part 5: Group B in the Center (two rounds; 50 minutes): Repeat Parts 2-4, with Group B as the inner circle and Group A as observer/coaches. Keep the same pairs since rapport has been built.

Part 6: Full Group Reflection (15 minutes): Gather together as a full group and reflect on what was learned from the exercise and the process of consultation.

1) What did you learn about yourself? What were your challenges? Did your ability to listen improve?
2) What did you learn about group consultation? Can you see using consultation to solve problems in the workplace?
3) Can you see how the communication skills you learned might help in difficult conversations?
4) What did you learn about the subject under discussion? Do you have a broader understanding of the topic? Were you influenced? Did you change your mind about anything?
5) Did the training help? Do you feel additional training would be beneficial?
6) How did this consultation compare with the earlier consultation? Did practicing the skills separately help to improve the capability?

e. Alternative method – Video Fishbowl[35]: Another way to achieve the benefits of the previous exercise that may save some time is to replace the inner and outer circles with videotaping. Both A and B groups can engage in separate consultations simultaneously. After 30 minutes, the teams exchange their videotapes for evaluation and feedback. After watching the other team's video, each team makes a presentation to the other team, highlighting what they observed and how consultation might be improved. After hearing from the other team, each team may wish to review their own video in light of what they heard to solidify learning. The advantage of the previous version, where each person is paired with a partner, is that each person can receive personal and direct feedback.

Promoting Unity in Diversity (p. 174 – 177)

Initial Reflection: Why is unity in diversity more enriching than unity in uniformity?

Discussion Questions:
1. How does back-biting create or contribute to disunity?
2. How does prejudice create or contribute to disunity?
3. How can appreciation of diversity help to address some of the systemic injustices in our society?
4. Why is unity in diversity especially necessary in the world today?
5. Is it possible to have effective consultation without this capability? Why or why not?
6. What attitudes promote unity in diversity and what attitudes hinder it? Why?

Group Activities:
1. *Understanding Barriers to Unity*: Identify an injustice that has contributed to disunity in your community or organization.
   a. Use the capability of consultation to identify root causes. Is there an unspoken "story" that is contributing to disunity?
   b. What are the assumptions that need to be examined?
   c. What are the harmful actions that stem from this?
   d. Is there back-biting?
   e. What actions can be taken to restore unity?
   f. Can you identify other capabilities that we have studied that can assist this process?
2. *Celebrating Diversity:* Put the names of each participant into a bowl.
   a. Pass the bowl around for each person to pick a name.
   b. Each one writes down how the person chosen contributes to the strength and beauty of the group by enhancing its diversity.
   c. Share thoughts in the group.

Group Reflection:
1. What did you learn?
2. Why does appreciation of diversity enhance unity?

3. What barriers must we overcome to celebrate diversity more effectively?
4. What actions can we take in our workplace and community?

Individual Reflection: Having participated in the group activities, think of how you can apply the learning as an individual.
1. Identify a situation in a group setting that has caused you pain and suffering. What happened? If you felt betrayed, what caused it?
2. In your life, if there is a situation where people are not getting along, can you better understand what is causing disunity?
3. Is there some way you may be contributing to it unconsciously? What are the unexamined assumptions?
4. What actions can you take to restore unity?

CAPABILITIES THAT CONTRIBUTE TO SOCIAL TRANSFORMATION

Establishing Justice (p. 179-182)

Initial Reflection: What can we do to contribute to the establishment of justice?

Discussion Questions:
1. Define justice.
2. Name four practices that contribute to social justice. Can you think of others?
3. Explain the relationship between oppression and ignorance. What are the practical implications of this relationship?
4. Explain the relationship between individual justice and social justice.

Group Reflection:
1. What can we do to help alleviate oppression caused by:
    a. ignorance of spiritual principles
    b. ignorance of laws and institutions responsible to ensure justice
    c. lack of skills and alternative options in life
2. What can we do to act more justly within our own organization?
3. How can we be sure that our institutional systems are not inherently discriminatory? How do we engage those that may feel marginalized to help us understand and address institutional bias?
4. In what ways do we each enjoy positions of privilege? How can we become more aware of our privileges and learn empathy with those who lack them?
5. What are the ways in which we each lack privilege?
6. How can we educate ourselves about the experience of the less privileged? What helps us develop empathy? What actions can we take?
7. How can we ensure that opportunities and access to resources are available to all?

Individual Reflection: Think of groups in the workplace or community that are frequently marginalized based on race, sex, nationality, ethnicity, etc.

1. What can we do personally to educate ourselves about their experience and learn empathy?
2. What kind of meaningful actions might we take that would be respectful and loving?
3. What are some practical ways we can become effective advocates and allies of those experiencing discrimination?

Transforming Dominating Relationships (p. 182-189)

Initial Reflection: Why are relationships based on collaboration more satisfying than relationships of domination?

Discussion Questions:

1. Give a concrete example of each of the types of relationship illustrated by Karlberg on page 183.
2. In your own words, explain the principles underlying the conceptual framework of relationships based on mutuality and collaboration.
3. How can a person in authority help those under his/her supervision to learn to participate in relationships based on mutuality and collaboration?
4. When we feel that someone is trying to dominate us, how can we most effectively try to transform the relationship?
5. Why is it useless to try to end domination by overthrowing those who are dominating?

Group Activities:
1. Role-play the following situations.
   a. A person who has traditionally been dominating takes steps to initiate the process of transforming his/her relationship with others.
   b. A person who is being dominated stands up to the dominator in a non-antagonistic way.
2. Think of a relationship in which you are either dominating or dominated. What can you do to transform that relationship?

Individual Reflection: Think of an intimidating relationship in your life.
1. Why do you feel intimidated? Are you responding to a dominating personality type or are you having feelings of self-doubt?
2. If the problem is external:
   a. Write down a conversation you might have using the listening and expression skills you learned in developing the capability of consultation in order to have an authentic exchange with this person.
   b. What risks are you taking? Are the risks real or imagined?
   c. If there is real risk with potential negative consequences, how will you protect yourself without putting the other person on the defensive? (Seek suggestions from others).
3. If the source of the problem is internal:
   a. Write down the "story" you are telling yourself. Highlight the judgmental statements.
   b. Rewrite (in a list) the statements you made about yourself. You will keep this to increase your awareness of your judgmental voice. Now cross out the highlighted sections in your story.
   c. What are your strengths? (You identified them in the capability of self-evaluation.)

d. Now write a new narrative that is objective and based on evidence. How will you overcome your challenges, using your strengths? What systematic process will you use to learn from your actions?
4. How might you re-engage in a mutually beneficial relationship? Write down the steps and the actions you will take to address this.

Empowering Education (p. 189-193)

Initial Reflection: How can we make educational activities more meaningful and enjoyable?

Discussion Questions:
1. What is "empowerment"? What does it mean to "empower through education"?
2. When is it important to transform mental models before presenting a new way of doing something?

Group Activities:
1. Plan a learning session that challenges prevalent mental models and identifies their flaws. Specify the activities you would use to:
    a. identify prevalent mental models,
    b. critically analyze those models, and
    c. adopt a conceptual framework aligned with evidence and values.
2. Plan a learning session to explore a capability that members of the group want to enhance.
    a. Identify a performance objective related to that capability (what you want the participants to be able to do at the end of the session).
    b. Identify 2 or more learning objectives needed to achieve the performance objective.

c. Plan activities for each of the four phases of the learning cycle (experience, reflection, conceptualization, application) that lead to achievement of one of the learning objectives.

Group discussion: It is important to appreciate that no matter how interesting and engaging an educational activity might be, it is only empowering if people walk away with tools to continually enhance their own learning. So, built into the process must be an accessible pathway for participants to become self-reliant regarding their own education.
1. Participating in a learning community is a very effective way to do this. Consult about how the group can become a vehicle for on-going learning.
2. What specific tools can facilitate the process of collective learning?
3. What tools might assist individual learning?

Elaborating a Principle-Based, Shared Vision (p. 194 – 197)

Initial Reflection: How can we create a shared vision based on values and principles?

Discussion Questions:
1. What is vision and how can a clear, inspiring vision contribute to more effective work?
2. What characteristics of a vision motivate others to act?
3. How can we help people to commit themselves to an institutional vision?
4. How can we help individuals to formulate their own personal vision and find resonance with the institutional vision?

Deepening our Understanding: Read Daniel Pink's book, *Drive: The Surprising Truth About What Motivates Us.* The author reviews research on motivation and concludes that having a lofty purpose, which a shared vision provides, is a much more powerful motivator than material incentives.

Group Activity: Help the group elaborate a shared vision using the following steps:
1. What is your dream for your institution? What inspires you? What would you like to see in the future? What does it look like? (As people speak, there are elements that will come into focus until consensus is reached.)
2. Identify the relevant principles.
3. List the priorities in the left-hand column of the table. (These should be principle-based.)
4. Utilize group consultation to fill in the other two columns of the table for each priority area.
5. From the last column, choose 3-5 of the most important priorities to incorporate in the vision.
6. Write a brief preliminary vision statement highlighting these goals.

A table like the one below might be helpful in carrying out this exercise. Examples of priority elements are given. However, those that emerge out of the group's consultation will more accurately reflect the vision of the group.

Shared Vision		
(incorporating shared principles)		
Priorities	**What have we achieved so far?**	**What will we achieve in _____ years? (Specify)**
Values-based & Evidence-based		
Sustainable		
Accessible to all		

Participatory		
Gender equity		
Culture of learning		
Diversity		

Transforming Institutions (p. 197-202)

Initial Reflection: How can an organization bring out the best in its members?

Discussion Questions:
1. Why is it important for an institution to have an explicit ethical framework?
2. What is the process an institution must traverse to embrace an ethical framework? How does this protect the institution in times of difficulty?
3. How does an institutional culture grow from this? How does it impact its members?
4. Give examples of the four stages of development of individuals and teams described by Kenneth Blanchard (p. 201) and how they relate to different types of supervision.
5. What are some of the characteristics of a learning organization? Why is each of these important?

Group Activity:
1. Evaluate to what degree your organization has the elements of an empowering institution:
    a. Clear values, vision and mission
    b. Alignment throughout the organization with the values, vision and mission

c. Congruence between a person's talents and capabilities and his/her responsibilities
   d. Opportunities for individual learning and developing capabilities
   e. Meaningful delegation and appropriate supervision
   f. Formalized systems for learning within the organization.
2. Choose two areas in which your organization wishes to improve, and set concrete goals and timelines for each.

Individual Reflection:
1. How can you help your organization become the best it can be?
2. How can you contribute to creating unity and justice?
3. What other actions could you take to enhance the health of your organization?

Understanding Historical Perspective (p. 202-205)

Initial Reflection: What does historical perspective have to do with creating a better world?

Discussion Questions:
1. Why is it beneficial for a group of people to know its own history?
2. How does knowledge of history put our efforts into perspective?
3. According to Toynbee, what importance does a creative minority play in the emergence of a new civilization?
4. What does civilization need today?
5. What contribution might our institution make to meeting the needs of the world?

Group Activities:
1. Identify stories from your cultural or religious heritage that inspire you – ones that you wish to transmit to the younger generations. How can this best be done?
2. Why is historical perspective essential for maturity?

3. How does historical perspective help us identify:
    a. Signs of danger, requiring caution and preparation?
    b. Opportunities for growth and sustainable development?
    c. Next steps to meet challenges and opportunities in proactive instead of reactive modes?
    d. How can we participate in the "creative minority" that assists our communities to meet challenges with maturity?
4. Choose a problem that exists in your community.
    a. What is the history of the problem? What are contributing factors? How does this understanding help to arrive at a solution?
    b. Indicate the transformative leadership capabilities that could contribute to its solution.
    c. Describe the way each capability might contribute.
    d. In what specific ways might you apply each capability?

Individual Reflection: Having historical perspective is not only relevant to institutions, but also to our own path in life. Reflect on what service life has prepared you for.
1. What is the meaning of your challenges and suffering?
2. What have you learned?
3. In what area is your contribution?
4. What is the gift you can offer to the world?

INTEGRATING THE CAPABILITIES

Transformative Leadership in the Family (p. 207-211)

Initial Reflection: How can we use our families as workshops in which to develop the capabilities of transformative leadership?

Discussion Questions:
1. Why is it important to practice transformative leadership capabilities in the family?
2. How can we base family life on principles?
3. How can parents help their children to become more responsible? More loving?
4. Why are family meetings useful?
5. Why is it important that parents spend time with each child individually and listen effectively to encourage his/her efforts?

Individual Reflection: The family provides the perfect opportunity to help children practice attitudes, qualities and skills that will help them become peacemakers and healers in the world, not to mention happier and more fulfilled individuals.
1. How can we help them to be free from the destructive effects of backbiting and prejudice?
2. How can we help them to participate effectively in consultation and develop skills of authentic communication?
3. How can we accompany them as they develop these and other capabilities?

Individual Activity: Make a time-specific plan, including at least 3 concrete actions that you can take to practice integrating the capabilities of transformative leadership in your family. Periodically evaluate your progress and set new goals and revise existing ones.

EPILOGUE

A Word About Ambition (p. 213-219)

Initial Reflection: Why is it better to be motivated by a desire to serve than by ambition?

Discussion Questions:
1. Why is it important to maintain a posture of humility, even when we have developed many of the capabilities of transformative leadership?
2. Explain how ambition and self-glorification undermine transformative leadership.
3. If we are not motivated by ambition, then what motivates us to practice transformative leadership and to work for social transformation?
4. Briefly explain the following qualities and explain how they counteract egocentric tendencies:
   a. modesty
   b. detachment
   c. impartiality
   d. purity of motive

Individual Reflection: Another way to check our attitude is to reflect on our inner state when things don't go our way. Perhaps we are striving hard for a specified outcome. The result may not be to our liking. Perhaps we were over-ruled or criticized, or the group just chose a different direction. Or perhaps the group has developed the capacity to move on without us. Reflect on how you might react.
1. Am I distressed that things turned out differently than I had hoped? Why?
2. Are my feelings hurt? Do I feel I have failed? Do I feel unjustly treated?
3. Why am I engaged in this process? What am I gaining? What are my motives?
4. How will I feel if the group succeeds but I get no acknowledgement for my role?

5. Am I willing to forego personal benefit in order for the group to achieve self-sufficiency or do I secretly wish to be indispensable?
6. Can I learn to derive satisfaction by witnessing growth and progress even if my role becomes increasingly irrelevant?

Individual Activity: Using the following chart, grade yourself weekly on a scale of 1 to 10 on the development of the qualities of modesty, detachment, impartiality, and purity of motive. You might also want to briefly write down the reasons for giving yourself the grade you do.

Qualities	Week 1	Week 2	Week 3	Week 4
Modesty				
Detachment				
Impartiality				
Purity of motive				

Developing the capabilities of transformative leadership is clearly a life-long process of learning, growth and improvement as we strive to better understand the vision and align our actions. If we cling uncompromisingly to a learning attitude in all we do, and revisit the learning cycle of action and reflection, we are sure to come closer to the vision of transformative leadership and make steady progress.

This guide, like the journey itself, is about learning. In this spirit, we would like to request all those who are engaged in utilizing these materials give us feedback, so that we can improve this guide. If you are forming a learning community and have found new ways of exploring these ideas, please share them with us so that we can all learn. Send your comments to mkhadem@northwestern.edu and juanitah48@gmail.com.

REFERENCES

[1] Appreciation to Rabbani Consulting, Salvador, Brazil for compiling some of these quotes. Others from Wikipedia, https://en.wikipedia.org/wiki/Golden_Rule

[2] Ervin Laszlo and Dalai Lama for the Club of Budapest, *Manifesto on the Spirit of Planetary Consciousness, 26 October 1996.* (http://www.clubofbudapest.org/clubofbudapest/index.php/en/about-us/the-manifesto-on-planetary-consciousness)

[3] Mozi (Ancient Chinese Philosopher), Wikipedia: https://en.wikipedia.org/wiki/Golden_Rule

[4] Confucius, *Analects* XV.24, tr. David Hinton (another translation is in the online Chinese Text Project) Wikipedia.

[5] Tao Te Ching, Chapter 49, Wikipedia: https://en.wikipedia.org/wiki/Golden_Rule#cite_note-54.

[6] Lu Hsiang Shan , (1139-1193) (Philosopher, Confucianism), *Complete Work of Lu Hsiang-shan, Wing-Tsit Chan, Chinese Philosophy*, Chapter 33

[7] *A Late Period Hieratic Wisdom Text: P. Brooklyn 47.218.135"*, Richard Jasnow, p. 95, University of Chicago Press, 1992, Wikipedia.

[8] Diogenes Laërtius, *The Lives and Opinions of Eminent Philosophers*, I:36, Wikipedia.

[9] Socrates, quoted in *Plato's Republic*

[10] *The Trial and Death of Socrates*, 3rd, Edition, translated by GMA Grube, Hacket Publishing Co, 2000

[11] Plato, *Apology: Crito and Phadeo of Socrates.*

[12] *Tirukkuṛaḷ,* Section on Virtue, Chapter 32.

[13] Vidura in *Mahabharata Shanti-Parva* 167:9.

[14] Guru Granth Sahib, quoted in *Anatheism: Returning to God After God* by Richard Kearney, Columbia University Press, 2010.

[15] Lord Mahavira, *Acaranga Sutra*, 24th Tirthankara, from Wikipedia.

[16] http://www.azquotes.com/quote/845815

[17] http://www.firstpeople.us/FP-Html-Wisdom/BlackElk.html

[18] *Mahābhārata Shānti-Parva* 167:9)

[19] Leviticus. *The Torah*. Jewish Publication Society. p. 19:17.

[20] Shabbath folio:31a, *Babylonian Talmud*

[21] *Pahlavi Texts of Zoroastrianism: The Dadistan-i Dinik*, Thomas Firminger Thiselton-Dyer (1843–1928), Forgotten Books (May 7, 2008), ISBN 978-1-60620-199-2.

[22] *Pahlavi Texts of Zoroastrianism: Shayast-na-Shayast*, Thomas Firminger Thiselton-Dyer (1843–1928), Forgotten Books (May 7, 2008), ISBN 978-1-60620-199-2

[23] *Tripitaka* (Buddhist Scripture), Udanavarga 5:18.

[24] *The Holy Bible, New Century Version*. 2005 by Thomas Nelson, Inc

[25] Al-Nawawi's Forty Hadiths

[26] Bahá'u'lláh, *Tablets of Bahá'u'lláh Revealed After Kitab-i-Aqdas*, Baha'i Publishing Trust, Wilmette, IL, p. 71.

[27] https://en.wikipedia.org/wiki/Towards_a_Global_Ethic:_An_Initial_Declaration; https://parliamentofreligions.org/pwr_resources/_includes/FCKcontent/File/TowardsAGlobalEthic.pdf

[28] Bahá'u'lláh, *Gleanings from the Writings of Bahá'u'lláh*, Baha'i Publishing Trust, Wilmette, IL, 1990, p. 346.

[29] Seligman, Martin EP, *Authentic Happiness: Using the New Positive Psychology to Realize Your Potential for Lasting Fulfillment*, Simon and Schuster, 2002

[30] Adapted by permission from Rabbani Consulting, Salvador, Brazil.

[31] Senge, Peter M, *The Fitfth Discipline: The Art and the Practice of the Learning Organization*, Crown Business, NY, 2010.

[32] Adapted by permission from Rabbani Consulting, Salvador, Brazil.

[33] Adapted from Peter Senge, *The Fifth Discipline Fieldbook*, Doubleday: NY, 1994, p. 384.

[34] Adapted from Peter Senge, *The Fifth Discipline Fieldbook*, Doubleday: NY, 1994, p. 396-8.

[35] Adapted from Peter Senge, *The Fifth Discipline Fieldbook*, Doubleday: NY, 1994, p. 399.

Printed in Great Britain
by Amazon